LIVING BY FAITH, NOT BY SIGHT

"Jesus said to him, 'If you can believe, all things are possible to him who believes.' "

Mark 9:23

LIVING BY
FAITH
NOT BY
SIGHT

K.P. YOHANNAN

BOOKS

a division of Gospel for Asia

www.gfa.org

Living by Faith, Not by Sight

© 2003 by K.P. Yohannan

All rights reserved.

ISBN: 978-1-59589-010-8

Published by gfa books, a division of Gospel for Asia
1800 Golden Trail Court, Carrollton, TX 75010 USA
phone: (972) 300-7777
fax: (972) 300-7778

Printed in the United States of America

For information about other materials, visit our website: *www.gfa.org*.

Table of Contents

Introduction

———

Knowing the Bible and being able to articulate that knowledge are not going to make your life, ministry or family situation improve. You can memorize the whole Bible and still live in defeat. You can raise your children according to biblical principles and still not see any fruit of that in their behavior and attitudes. In an example familiar to many, you can write hundreds of letters asking people for financial support, but adequate funds may not come in. Something is wrong; faith is missing.

As you read the pages of this booklet, please keep in mind the verse found in Hebrews 4:2—"But the word which they heard did not profit them, not being mixed with faith in those who heard it." There's a chemistry to take place. For example, when hydrogen is mixed with oxygen in the presence of heat, a chemical reaction takes place and water is produced. Two separate elements, when combined, yield an entirely different result than if they were never mixed. This is true in life as well. There's a chemistry that needs to occur in our lives—in what we see, hear and know being mixed with faith. You may have needs or promises from God, but if they are never mixed with the element of faith, you will never see the reaction take place to bring those to fruition. *All things are possible to him who believes!*" (Mark 9:23).

CHAPTER ONE

Mixed with Faith

Perhaps you have enjoyed standing back and watching somebody else who has stepped out on the tremendous reality of faith. Maybe you rejoiced and thanked God for what He did for them through faith. But when the time came for your faith to be tested, what did you do? Did you respond according to faith or sight? As you find yourself pressing on to live this life pleasing to the Lord, in joy, peace and purpose, do you live by faith, confident that He who began the good work in you will be faithful to complete it (see Philippians 1:6)?

By nature, we are people who like to work things through for ourselves. We like to think we did it. We like to feel strong, able and competent in handling our problems. We have our images to keep intact. We say spiritual words and read all sorts of good Christian books to help us in this endeavor. We consult pastors, Christian counselors and well-intentioned friends, seeking their wisdom and trying to do what they suggest. We may have heard a thousand times that to walk with the Lord requires brokenness and humility, but in finding ways to work on life's problems by ourselves, we live in pride. We'd rather trust our methods of "perfecting" ourselves rather than have faith in God.

Our own solutions never work—they never worked for me and they will never work for you. The real solution to the variety of situations we face in life will only come by faith. Hebrews 11:6 says, "Without faith it is impossible to please [God]." God works by faith. Unless all that we know, all that we have heard in church services and in the books we've read is mixed with faith, it isn't worth anything. The Bible cannot save anyone. The Bible cannot set you free from sickness or demon-possession. The Bible cannot provide your funds. Knowledge of the Bible will not make you a better person. Knowing the Scriptures didn't help the Pharisees. Don't fool yourself. Satan can quote Scriptures more fluently than any of us.

In speaking of the Israelites as they came for the first time to the border of the Promised Land, Hebrews 4:2 says, "For indeed the gospel was preached to us as well as to them; *but the word which they heard did not profit them, not being mixed with faith in those who heard it*"(emphasis added). This Scripture is referring to God's people. They knew the Word. They knew the promises. But still, they died out in the wilderness. This happened not because they didn't know what God wanted for them, but because they didn't mix all their knowledge with faith.

That is the reason why, although God had promised them the land, He did not bring them into that promise. The Israelites came to the border of the Promised Land, but they couldn't enter because of their unbelief. They saw the giants in the land. They saw the fortified cities. They saw the impossibilities. And 10 of the spies said (paraphrase), "We simply cannot do it." These spies were telling the truth. They were not lying. They could not do it; the armies of Israel were just not strong enough. Joshua and Caleb, the two spies who brought back a different report, believing they would see victory, did not argue with the others about the impossibilities. They did not say, "You bunch of liars, be quiet." No. Instead they replied, "If the LORD delights in us, then

11

He will bring us into this land and give it to us, 'a land which flows with milk and honey' " (Numbers 14:8). Through faith, Joshua and Caleb knew that God was able, and that made all the difference.

Faith is still what makes the difference today. I am constantly amazed when I see beautiful, childlike faith in action. I can hardly believe it when I read letters from simple Hindus, Muslims and Buddhists who know hardly anything about the Bible. They write and say, "I believed what you said on the radio, and this is what God did. So now we believe in Jesus too."

One particular family who was listening to one of our broadcasts heard that "Jesus can do anything." At the time, this family had a sick goat. Do you know what they did? I love this. It's such childlike faith, so simple, so believing. They took the radio and placed it on the sick goat, believing that the Jesus they heard about through the radio could heal the goat. Sure enough, their goat got up and walked around, completely healed!

Please understand—nobody tells these people to do these sorts of things. They hear about Jesus, that He loves them, that He died for them, that He does miracles—and they simply believe. Their faith is so unquestioning. "God said it. Jesus is able. So I believe."

And it works! Logic cannot explain it and I cannot explain it, other than the truth that "according to your faith let it be to you" (Matthew 9:29). Yet what is seemingly so simple can be extremely difficult for a lot of us. We like to understand how things work, and we take pride in our ability to figure things out. But the realm of faith does not dwell in logic and formulas.

How can we grow in the mountain-moving faith that we read about in the pages of our Bible—stories of Daniel in the lion's den and the little boy David with his sling? The answer is found in God's Word. Romans 10:17 says, "Faith comes by hearing, and hearing by the word of God." The purpose of God's Word is to help grow our faith in Almighty God and His promises. When we know His promises and believe Him, taking Him at His Word, we walk in victory. Faith is the victory!

CHAPTER TWO

A Deeper Understanding

During my seminary years in the United States, my Greek professor was Dr. McBeth, a brilliant man with great understanding and insight into the Greek language. He taught us how to study the Bible in light of the rich meaning of the original Greek. It was amazing how he would take passages from Scripture and unfold before us the wonder and depth of them. For example, let me give you a little background of the original Greek word for *faith* in the Bible. We run into a linguistic misunderstanding with the word *faith* when we deal with it in the English language.

In biblical text, two words are commonly used: *faith*, which is a noun and *believe*, which is a verb. If you look at these words in their English form, there is no obvious connection between the two. This makes us think that we are dealing with two different concepts. As a result, when we study the Bible or preach, we make a distinction between the words *believing* and having *faith*.

However, in the Greek language there is no such distinction made. For the noun *faith*, the Greek word is *pisitis*. For the verb *to believe*, the word is *pisteuo*. The verb is formed directly from the noun. The stem of each word is from the same four letters: P-I-S-T. Our English words for faith and believe come from the same Greek root word.

As far as the Greek is concerned, believing is simply exercising faith. Conversely, exercising faith is believing. This is clearly portrayed in Jesus' dialogue with the two blind men in Matthew 9:28–29: "And when He had come into the house, the blind men came to Him. And Jesus said to them, 'Do you *believe* that I am able to do this?' They said to Him, 'Yes, Lord.' Then He touched their eyes, saying, 'According to your *faith* let it be to you' " (emphasis added).

We see the connection again as Jesus addresses Peter and the other disciples in Mark 11:22–23. "So Jesus answered and said to them, 'Have *faith* in God. For assuredly, I say to you, whoever says to this mountain, "Be removed and be cast into the sea," and does not doubt in his heart, but *believes* that those things he says will be done, he will have whatever he says' " (emphasis added). In all these Scripture portions, you can see that believing and having faith are the same exact thing.

In English, the opposite of belief is unbelief. The prefix "un" makes it the opposite. But to make the opposite in Greek, the prefix "a" is added, turning *pisitis* (faith) into *apisitis* (unfaith). In English we don't have unfaith; we simply just call it unbelief. And *apisitis* (unfaith) translates into English as unbelief. Also connected with this four-letter stem, P-I-S-T, we have the adjective *pistos*, which means faithful or believing. From the opposite of this, using the prefix "a," we have *apistos*, meaning unfaithful or unbelieving. All these different words with the same P-I-S-T stem occur hundreds of times in the New Testament.

If you examine these verses, you will find a massive, powerful theme ordained by God: Faith is the key to experiencing all that God has promised. This strong and pervasive theme saturates the entire teachings of the New Testament Scripture. In English, we do not see it clearly because it is fractured into two separate parts. But God has given us faith, or believing Him, as the single most necessary thing for living a life of all that He has promised. That one Greek word from the stem P-I-S-T is central to the revelation of Jesus Christ in the New Testament as Savior, Healer and Provider.

CHAPTER THREE

Faith Defined

In Hebrews 11:1 we find the definition of faith: "Now faith is the substance of things hoped for, the evidence of things not seen." The NIV translation says, "Now faith is being sure of what we hope for and certain of what we do not see."

What does Scripture say that faith is? First, it says that faith is the substance. It is being sure of whatever it is that we hope for. Faith is so real it is called substance. Substance is the material of which something is made, the building blocks of it. Your faith is the substance, the building blocks of God's promises! The Greek word used for this particular word substance is *hupostasis*. *Hupostasis* means "that which stands under," the basis of something or that which supports the thing.

To understand further, we can look at the other ways the word, substance, or *hupostasis*, is used in the Bible. In Hebrews 1:3 NASB it says, "He [Jesus] is the radiance of His glory and the exact representation of His nature." The Greek word used here for nature is the same word, substance or *hupostasis*. In other words, this verse is saying that God, who is eternal and invisible, became visible—became of substance—in Jesus Christ. Jesus is the exact representation of the Invisible, Almighty God. The substance—Jesus—is the real God in human form. Just like Jesus is the substance of God who is invisible, faith is the substance of those things that we hope for that are invisible.

From the second part of Hebrews 11:1, we see that faith is the "evidence of things not seen." In a courtroom, the judge and jury expect to see some type of evidence proving that whatever a person is charged with is indeed true. The evidence presented determines the outcome of the case. Your faith is also the evidence, determining the outcome of what you are believing for.

Faith directly relates to the invisible, to things that we cannot see with our eyes or handle with our senses. When I was learning about faith years ago, this was the place where the Lord first opened my eyes—that my five senses, no matter how hard I try, will not be able to explain faith or put it into practice and use. Faith is not dealing with what I can see with my eyes or touch with my hands. For example, consider the verse in Acts 16:31, "Believe on the Lord Jesus Christ, and you will be saved." I don't know how to figure this out. How in the world, with my natural senses, can I just believe and be saved? It is totally outside of my logic and my senses, something I cannot comprehend with my mind. Our senses only relate to this visible world. But faith takes us beyond the visible to the invisible, to the underlying reality by which the whole universe was formed, which is by the Word of God. Hebrews 11:3 says, "By faith we understand that the worlds were framed by the word of God, so that the things which are seen were not made of things which are visible."

God and His Word

Faith deals exclusively with believing God and His Word. It is with this foundation that biblical faith is distinguished from all else. We may say, "Oh, I believe in that politician. I believe this make of car. I believe in this medicine because it worked for me." This kind of belief is based on our past experience, what we have seen with our eyes or understood with our minds. Unlike this type of belief, the faith that brings about the promises of God is powerful only because of whom the faith is placed in.

God's very nature and character is faithfulness and goodness. He is always constant and true. So is His Word. Neither He nor His Word will ever change. "For I am the Lord, I do not change" (Malachi 3:6). And God watches over His Word to make sure it comes to pass. Isaiah 55:10–11 says: "For as the rain comes down, and the snow from heaven, and do not return there, but water the earth, and make it bring forth and bud, that it may give seed to the sower and bread to the eater, so shall My word be that goes forth from My mouth; it shall not return to Me void, but it shall accomplish what I please, and it shall prosper in the thing for which I sent it."

Because of this truth, we can confidently believe God, knowing that He does not change, that He is full of goodness and that what He said in His Word will happen!

True Faith

Faith is not denying what is happening in your life or what you are experiencing. It is not pretending that you do not see the dangers or the problems before you. Like I mentioned earlier, Caleb and Joshua saw the strength of those who inhabited the Promised Land. They did not deny that the cities were fortified or that the giants were real. Faith is not denying that you are sick when you are horribly ill. It is not denying that your finances have run short when you are out of funds. Rather, faith is seeing all the problems before you with your earthly eyes, yet not using those eyes to see the solution.

God is greater than every difficult situation we face. Faith sees God for who He is, for His ability and for His promises, and believes on Him in the midst of all the difficulties known. By faith we are able to look beyond the problems and solutions of man to see Him who is invisible and can do the impossible!

Do It God's Way

From the world's perspective, faith often looks foolish and illogical. But faith trusts God to do what He has promised, no matter how foolish the steps He asks us to take may seem. There is nothing of man's way in faith. Faith led David to face a giant with a simple slingshot and five stones (see 1 Samuel 17). Faith led Joshua to command a makeshift army to walk around a walled city, blowing trumpets and shouting for their victory (see Joshua 6). Please put yourself in these men's place for a moment and realize how humbling or frightening these things must have been. But remember, no matter how foolish or ridiculous Joshua and the children of Israel looked while walking around the city of

Jericho for seven days, it was by their faith that the walls did come down! In the end, faith always wins out!

In 2 Kings 5 the story is told of Naaman the leper who was sent to Elisha the prophet to be healed of his leprosy. When he arrived at the prophet's door, Naaman was told, "Go and wash in the Jordan seven times, and your flesh shall be restored to you, and you shall be clean" (v. 10).

But Naaman didn't like that solution. The Jordan River was just some distant, muddy water to him. In verses 11–12 we are told that "Naaman became furious, and went away and said, 'Indeed, I said to myself, "He will surely come out to me, and stand and call on the name of the Lord his God, and wave his hand over the place, and heal the leprosy." Are not the Abanah and the Pharpar, the rivers of Damascus, better than all the waters of Israel? Could I not wash in them and be clean?' So he turned and went away in a rage."

The ways of God seemed foolish to Naaman—so much so that he stormed away from the prophet's home, still a leper. Naaman responded with human logic. He thought he knew the best way for his healing to happen, and when he heard something as foolish as dipping in some distant river, he wouldn't accept it. Just when he was about to return home, his servants met him saying, " 'If the prophet had told you to do something great, would you not have done it? How much more then, when he says to you, "Wash, and be clean"?' So he went down and dipped seven times in the Jordan, according to the saying of the man of God; and his flesh was restored like the flesh of a little child, and he was clean" (2 Kings 5:13–14).

When we do it God's way, believing Him above the ways of man and our own reasoning, we will see the power of God at work and will receive the promises of God. Remember that "God has chosen the foolish things of the world to put to shame the wise" (1 Corinthians 1:27).

It Is Simple

Jesus says, "Unless you are converted and become as little children, you will by no means enter the kingdom of heaven" (Matthew 18:3). Little children believe with reckless abandon. If a father tells his son to jump from a burning, two-story building, the son will jump. He will not stand there and think about physics and gravity and calculate if his father is strong enough to catch him. He doesn't reason with logic and think, "I might hurt myself. Maybe I should look for another way down." No. He simply jumps in faith. Someone he trusts said to do it, so the son jumps and is saved. We need to be like this— trusting God so completely, so confidently.

We must learn to lean on His understanding rather than our own (see Proverbs 3).

A complex, reasoned faith doesn't cure leprosy, kill giants or cause walls to crumble. A complex faith only imprisons us in a maze of theological wonderland. I am not saying to run out and do things that don't make sense. I am not saying to think of some ridiculous thing you want and believe for it. Some extreme groups preach this false kind of faith. They say just pray it and claim it and God will send an angel to bring the Rolls Royce or whatever elaborate thing you may want. That is not faith—it is madness. That is feeding the desires of the flesh in the name of faith. You can't use faith to get what you want for yourself. Faith only brings to you what God wants for you.

Have faith in God—the kind of faith that David had, the faith that defeats huge giants with simple stones. Let God do what He has promised to do. Listen to what He says in His Word and follow it. Even if you can't understand it fully, do it. Don't be like Naaman and let your reasoning postpone the promises of God at work in your life. Believe Him and step out in faith. Faith throws itself onto God and holds Him to His character and His Word. Faith never fails because God never fails.

CHAPTER FOUR

By Faith, Not Sight

———

Second Corinthians 5:7 says, "For we walk by faith, not by sight." Here we see that there is a clear distinction between faith and sight. The two are opposites; each excludes the other. When we walk by faith, we don't have to worry about how things look. If we walk by sight, there is no room for faith. We can see where we are going and so we simply follow the path we see. If you know how something is going to happen or know how to solve your problems on your own, you don't need faith. You don't need God if you can work it out without Him. But the truth is we always need God. Thus, we must always live by faith.

But in this quest to live by faith, we run into the very real conflict between our old nature and our new nature. There is a continual war between the two—the flesh and the Spirit, the temporal and the eternal, the walking by sight and the walking by faith. Our old nature demands to see, to experience, to understand. But the new nature is different. It is able to believe without seeing and feeling, because God has created that new nature in us.

We are a culture that demands to see proof. Scientists spend years running experiments just to show that some medicine or treatment works. Much like Thomas, who wouldn't believe the Lord Jesus had risen until he put his hand in His pierced side, we find it hard to believe anything we cannot see, declaring "seeing is believing." Please, let us not be like this. Jesus said in John 20:29, "Blessed are those who have not seen and yet have believed."

The Bible shows us a way of life that isn't dependent on only what we can see. Psalm 27:13 says, "I would have lost heart, unless I had *believed* that I would see the goodness of the Lord in the land of the living" (emphasis added). Matthew 21:22 says, "And whatever things you ask in prayer, *believing*, you will receive" (emphasis added). Acts 16:31 says, "*Believe* on the Lord Jesus Christ, and you will be saved, you and your household" (emphasis added). In each of these passages, which comes first, believing or seeing? Believing, of course! First we believe and then we see! So, if you want to see something happen, start believing. Stop trying to see it first.

In John 11 there is the story of Lazarus, Jesus' close friend who died. Martha, Lazarus's sister, was crushed inside by the death of her brother, as I'm sure anyone would be. At the same time, it also seemed that she was a bit upset with Jesus. In John 11:20–21 we read, "Now Martha, as soon as she heard that Jesus was coming, went and met Him, but Mary was sitting in the house. Now Martha said to Jesus, 'Lord, if You had been here, my brother would not have died.' " But Jesus answered Martha by gently reminding her, "Did I not say to you that if you would *believe* you would see the glory of God?" (John 11:40, emphasis added).

Martha was focused on the natural and concentrating on the facts. When Jesus had finally arrived on the scene, Lazarus had been dead for four days. There would be an odor assuring everyone of that fact. But Jesus said (paraphrase), "Please don't look at the facts, only believe. Believe first and then you will see." We cannot figure this out—yet we don't always need to. God requires nothing but our belief, even if it is only as small as a mustard seed. Have you ever seen a mustard seed? They are incredibly small, like a tiny little speck, the smallest seed of all plants! Even faith just that small, Jesus said, is able to move mountains! "I tell you the truth, if you have faith as small as a mustard seed, you can say to this mountain, 'Move from here to there' and it will move. Nothing will be impossible for you" (Matthew 17:20, NIV). Even when believing is difficult, He wants us to cry out, as the man with the epileptic son did, and say, "Lord, I believe; help my unbelief!" (Mark 9:24).

In Waiting

Abraham didn't walk by faith to obtain the promised son until it became clear that walking by sight with his own plans guiding him just wouldn't accomplish the purposes of God. God had promised Abraham and Sarah a son, and they had waited a long time for the fulfillment of that promise. As time went by, it seemed nothing was ever going to happen, and both of them grew impatient. This inspired Sarah to think of a plan: Abraham could lay with Hagar the maidservant and receive the promised son that way. In Genesis 16:2 we read that Abraham "heeded the voice of Sarai," listening to the voice of his wife rather than the voice of God. He lay with Hagar and, sure enough, she bore the son Ishmael. But this was a plan of the flesh to bring about the plan of God—and that will never work.

Later on, in Genesis 17:18–19, it says, "And Abraham said to God, 'Oh, that Ishmael might live before You!' Then God said: 'No, Sarah your wife shall bear you a son, and you shall call his name Isaac; I will establish My covenant with him for an everlasting covenant, and with his descendants after him.' " God basically said to Abraham, "Yes, you got yourself a son, but no, I cannot bless a product of the flesh. Live by faith and let Me do it My way."

Until Abraham didn't know how to get a child, he didn't need faith. He walked by sight first, obtaining Ishmael, but he was not the son God had promised. Only when it was completely impossible—when both he and Sarah were too old and when their schemes to get a child their own way had failed—did Abraham have the faith to let God do it His way.

Most examples of the futility of walking by sight aren't so clear as this one. You can make your life look spiritual by obeying the Ten Commandments and the Sermon on the Mount. You can walk by sight and it can look okay, even good. Mahatma Gandhiji, the father of my nation, was known as a man who literally obeyed the Sermon on the

Mount. When he died (as seen in the movie *Gandhi)*, the last thing he said, translated in English, was, "O God!" But that translation can be deceiving. Gandhi was not calling out "O God!" to the God of the Sermon on the Mount or the God of the Ten Command-ments, which he was so known for following. He was actually calling out *"Hare Ram"* or "O God!" to lord Ram, the Hindu god whom he followed. Even though Gandhi knew the good things Jesus said and even followed them, he still had no faith in Jesus Christ to save him. He walked by sight, by the good things he did, never having faith for salvation.

With deliberate willpower, people can rightly obey the laws and modify their be-havior. This was the case with the story in Luke 18 of the rich young ruler who obeyed the Ten Commandments. He was the model individual, but just because he was perfect in obedience doesn't mean he lived by faith. The Bible says, "Whatever is not from faith is sin" (Romans 14:23). "Sin" is walking your own road, regardless of whether the road you choose looks good or bad to the rest of society.

Even today, a lot of Christian work is done by sight. There are Christian people who think they know how to carry out God's work. They think they know how to win the lost, grow fruitful ministries or attract the youth. But the truth is that if what you are doing is not done by faith, God will not bless it. God is deeply concerned that we do His work, His way, by faith. It is simply how things function in the kingdom of God.

Looking to God to Accomplish

Sometimes walking by faith seems passive and slow in coming to pass. Look at David's life. In the book of 1 Samuel, we can see how David endured much, yet he never resorted to fighting to make sure the crown God promised him would be his. He had faith that God would fulfill the promises He had made.

David started out as a mere child taking care of his father's sheep. On the day the prophet Samuel came to anoint the new king, chosen from David's family, his own father didn't even regard young David as one to be considered. It wasn't until Samuel had passed over all the older sons that David's name was even mentioned. Then, when David was finally acknowledged and Samuel poured the oil on David's head, anointing him as the chosen king, what did David do? Go and demand the crown and begin reigning? Not at all! He went right back to his simple sheep-herding.

It was only later, when David brought food to his brothers who were fighting the Philistines, that God showed His favor upon him, giving David the victory to defeat Goliath. When King Saul found out about this, he didn't step down right then and say, "Alright David, now you are the king." No. David's journey of obtaining the promise from God was, from then on, filled with dodging spears, running for his life and living in caves in the wilderness, hungry and destitute. Even David's wife gave up on him, and several times his band of followers threatened to leave. Once he even had to pretend to be a madman just to escape his adversaries.

Finally, after many years, David had the upper hand. King Saul, unattended and alone, came into the cave where David was hiding. This was David's opportunity to kill the king who had so earnestly sought his life, or at least to capture him! All those years of running could finally come to an end. Saul's life was in David's hand and at his mercy. But God did not want David to act on the opportunity this way. The temptation to walk by sight must have been so great. Yet trusting in God and not choosing his own ways, David allowed Saul to escape so that God could fulfill the promise of making him king in His own way and in His own timing.

Even after this incident, Saul didn't change. He was soon after David once more. This time God caused a deep sleep to come upon Saul's army, making it possible for David and his men to walk right up and take the spear from near the sleeping king's head. The men with David urged him to kill Saul. One said (paraphrase), "God has delivered Saul into your hands. What are you waiting for? Weren't you praying that God would fulfill His promise that He made to you? And here he is, just one jab with the spear and you can kill him!"

To strike Saul at this point would not have required scheming or conniving on David's part at all. There would have been no manipulation or tricks. But still David would not do it. He would not do it because he believed God and His way of bringing things about. This journey of trusting God was not a one- or two-year struggle. It went on for many years. But David continued to live by faith, not by sight, choosing God's way above his own.

Now take that into your world. Take David's example of living by faith and apply it to your situation. I am saying this to you so that you will continue to lay aside your cleverness, abilities and intelligence. We must choose to walk by faith, trusting God to fulfill His promise in His way and timing.

I have my own experiences and lessons the Lord has taught me in choosing to walk by faith, trusting Him rather than my ability. For example, things don't always go the way

I would like them to in some of my meetings. I remember distinctly a couple of past experiences while speaking in churches, when, toward the end of my message, I would think to myself, "If only I could just say a few more persuasive words. If only I could present the need in this particular way, then I could get the job done. I could get that fruitful response. I could see them make that commitment." But in those times, I also clearly remember how in my heart I felt, "If I say one more thing I will be operating in the realm of sight. I will be manipulating. I will be forcing it. If I say that, I will be using my God-given ability to convince people. I may get the job done, but it will be nothing but another Ishmael, my way of producing what God promised." And I back off. By God's grace, I let it go.

Seeing Things That Are Not Seen

In 2 Corinthians 4:17–18 Paul says, "For our light affliction, which is but for a moment, is working for us a far more exceeding and eternal weight of glory, while we do not look at the things which are seen, but at the things which are not seen. For the things which are seen are temporary, but the things which are not seen are eternal."

The momentary and light afflictions that Paul spoke of weren't easy, little problems. No!

What he called "momentary and light" were big things—being shipwrecked, beaten, stoned and whipped! He was cold, imprisoned and hungry (see 2 Corinthians 11). Yet he called these afflictions "light" and "but for a moment." He could say this because compared to the eternal weight of glory, they were just that—pale in comparison to what they were producing in him. Paul knew that the hardships were working in him something good and of great weight that would last forever.

There is a paradox, too, in what Paul is saying. How can we look at things that we don't see? In 2 Corinthians 4:18 he writes, "[We look at] the things which are not seen." How does that work? It's like a man who is blind saying that he is "going to see a movie." How can you see things that you don't have the natural ability to see? We find the answer in the example of Moses, for this is exactly what he did and what kept him trusting. "By faith he left Egypt, not fearing the king's anger; *he persevered because he saw him who is invisible*" (Hebrews 11:27, NIV, emphasis added). It's that gaze—that looking to Christ—which gives us the grace to persevere in our journey of faith.

When I am faced with problems, disappointments, lack of resources or sickness, if I fix my eyes on the things that are visible, then all those difficulties discourage me and I get weighed down by the impossibilities. But when I turn my eyes to the invisible, fixing them on God, all those difficulties become instruments He uses to help me live by faith.

By faith, those afflictions are used to change me on the inside so that I reflect His glory. These pains and hardships will lead to the benefits and rewards that He promised, if I would only trust Him in the situations of life. But if I do not keep my eyes focused beyond the problems, beyond the struggles and beyond the here and now and on God, then those promises will not come about, simply because I am not putting my faith to work.

I remember back to when I was 16 years old serving with Operation Mobilization. It was there that I first began to understand that every disagreement, every problem, every tension, every irritation happens in our lives because God has orchestrated it. He has designed it. God put us in that situation or with that person so that we would be changed into His image. You may say, "I don't want this kind of problem." But He has designed it just for you, to be an instrument to make you more like Him.

The team I was on during this time consisted of eight or nine people from all different parts of India. We all had different ways of doing things, and it was very difficult for us to get along. It was so bad that some days we couldn't even be involved in outreach ministry because of the disagreements we had with one another. But one day, as we were all fighting and arguing, our leader explained to the team the lessons found in the life of Jacob and his experience with his uncle, Laban.

Jacob was a smart, shrewd, very cunning individual, his name originally meaning "deceiver." Jacob tricked his father to get his own brother's birthright and blessing. After doing this, he ran away from his father's house to stay with his uncle, Laban. I'm sure Jacob thought that he had made a clean getaway, safely hiding out with his uncle. But you know what happened? For the 20 years Jacob lived with Laban, he got the same medicine of deceit and trickery that he dished out to his father and brother. God put Jacob with someone just like himself to create a broken and contrite heart in him. God wanted repentance and humility to replace the scheming and greed. And God used that difficult individual, Laban, to change Jacob's heart so he would become the man God wanted.

We need to recognize the purposes of God in placing difficult individuals or situations in our lives. We must see that it is through these adverse circumstances, like lack of food or funding, that we are able to experience the miracles of God. We have to see beyond the visible and look at the things that are invisible. This is what it means to live by faith. See your life through the eyes of faith and let God use the difficult things for your eternal betterment, for your blessing and for His glory. This is what He has promised, and this is what He will do.

By faith we can embrace difficulties rather than despise them. This is the message given in James 1:2–4. "My brethren, count it all joy when you fall into various trials, knowing that the testing of your faith produces patience. But let patience have its perfect work, that you may be perfect and complete, lacking nothing." By faith you can say, "Lord, I thank You that You have put me with this difficult individual. I thank You for these adverse circumstances. Lord, You knew all this long before I was born. You put me here. You have something on Your mind. You want to do something through these hard situations that I cannot see. I submit, Lord. I don't want to fight. Take it and work it for Your eternal purpose."

Just Like Jesus

Regarding His death on the cross, Jesus said, "Shall I not drink the cup which My Father has given Me?" (John 18:11). Do you notice whom the cup was from? Jesus knew that Pilate hadn't given Him the cup. He knew that the Jewish people hadn't given Him the cup. He knew that the cup had not been given Him by Judas. Jesus called it, "the cup which *My Father* has given Me." This was a cup of suffering and sacrifice of the greatest and most difficult kind, designed specifically by God for His own precious Son! Jesus recognized this and knew this. And because of that He was able to see beyond the natural to the eternal, infinite purposes of God. Can we say that with our little problems? When we can, then we are truly living by faith. Everything that comes our way comes only by God's approval, and He only approves of things that are meant for our eternal benefit.

Rest assured; God has a plan even in the midst of tears and tension. Look at the faith of those in Hebrews 11. There we read of miraculous healings and amazing victories. But please don't miss the fact that the road to those victories was paved with great persever-ance, in the face of persecution and intense difficulties. God knows what is best for us, and He knows how to perfectly work in us His very own character, giving us the strength to endure the process. In every situation and with every hard-to-deal-with individual, He is "working for us a far more exceeding and eternal weight of glory" (2 Corinthians 4:17). When we live in the reality of this truth, we are able to accept with joy whatever He brings into our lives because we trust Him.

CHAPTER FIVE

Seeing Him Who Is Invisible

———

Hebrews 11:27 says, "By faith [Moses] forsook Egypt, not fearing the wrath of the king; for he endured as seeing Him who is invisible." Oftentimes when we read these Bible verses, we skip over them so fast, never really understanding the struggles these people went through. Moses *endured.* Do you realize what he endured? They were not easy things. Moses first had to deal with the fact that what he had known as his "family" indeed was not. Then he forsook everything that was given to him—the robes, the title, the honor, the food and the riches—to become numbered among his own people, the slaves of the day. Moses then had to flee into the desert and become a lowly shepherd for years. The only reason he persevered for 40 years in that hot, dry place that wasn't his home was because he saw "Him who is invisible."

And Moses continued to endure all his life. Chosen by God, Moses was sent to challenge the greatest empire and leader in his world at the time. He came against Pharaoh—the guy he grew up with, whom he once knew as his brother—not just once, but numerous times. Pharaoh wasn't exactly happy about his authority being challenged. Yet Moses continued to endure until He saw the promises of God.

Only faith can enable us to live like that and to see those things done that others consider impossible. Moses' faith gave him sight and set his hope on what God promised. Faith let him see beyond the realm of the natural into the realm of the supernatural, where God dwells and operates.

When we face struggles, problems and needs, it is easy to get discouraged. We want to give up the battle because the natural man tells us the problem is too big. I know this because it happens to me. But we cannot endure in this life without faith. We cannot endure unless we choose to see the invisible. My precious brothers and sisters, please fix your eyes on Him who is invisible. Be certain of what you do not see, "hold fast the confession of

[your] hope without wavering, for He who promised is faithful" (Hebrews 10:23).

Can It Be Done?

One afternoon, 10 or 15 years ago, an incredible thing happened. My wife, Gisela, and I, along with some staff members, were sitting in McDonalds reminiscing on our days with Operation Mobilization when we'd travel all over the place in vans, preaching the Gospel and seeing hundreds come to Christ.

All of a sudden, in the midst of our conversation, it was as though there was a burst of energy and hope. Remembering those "good old days" and the ministry we were able to do by traveling in vans got me thinking. In the midst of all the reminiscing and dreaming, I said out loud, "Why can't we believe God for 100 vehicles to go forth and preach the Gospel and win millions to Jesus Christ?" If you knew our financial budget at the time, you'd understand how absolutely crazy and ridiculous this idea was! There was just no way we could make that happen. We're talking 100 vehicles, at $12,000 to $15,000 per vehicle!

I remember that day so clearly. Right there at the table, I pulled out my wallet and opened it up. I only had about four one-dollar bills in my wallet. I took them out and, with my red felt pen that was in my pocket, I wrote on those dollar bills "the first down payment, by faith, toward buying 100 vehicles," believing the Lord that these vehicles would be fully equipped with everything needed to preach the Gospel. Right there in McDonalds, we laid our hands on the dollar bills and prayed, saying, "Lord, we are just helpless people, but we want to believe You, the great God who owns the whole world. You can do it. And this is our first down payment as a commitment to believe You for these 100 vehicles."

When we got back to the office, I gave Margaret, the woman who handles our finances, those four dollar bills. I told her, "Please don't spend this money yet, but put it in an envelope and keep it." Until this day, the money is still sitting in that envelope, marked with my handwriting the date and the time when we first committed those four dollar bills to the miracle of God.

Do you know what soon happened? Before we even had time to tell this to anyone, money began to come in for vehicles! Today we now have well over 100 vehicles, plus enough money for more. How did that happen? From the days of my old reasoning, I would have said, "This is absolutely insane!" But God has chosen the "foolish" things and His ways above the smart, wise and logical things of our world. Anything is possible with our God!

His Promises Are True

When my children, Danny and Sarah, were growing up, I used to struggle with what would happen to them in the American culture. I was afraid they would get sidetracked from the faith. I would tell Gisela, "We must relocate to India. I don't want to live in America. Our children are going to be lost here. This country will ruin them." I even remember thinking that it was better not to have children in America than to have children and see them drift away.

Some people see me as a man of faith. But in this issue, all the faith was up in my head where it wasn't doing any good. I was focusing only on what I could see, not walking by faith. I had a bunch of knowledge in my head, but it was not alive or active. James 2:20 talks about this kind of faith. "But do you want to know, O foolish man, that faith without works is dead?" I lived with a lot of agony because I wouldn't step out on faith and let God fulfill His promises in Danny's and Sarah's lives.

It was in those times that Gisela would remind me of how she grew up, saying, "But I was born in Germany. I was raised in a culture like this, and God protected me and preserved me. I believe my children will not be lost. I believe God will watch over them. I believe His promises are true for them." But it was so hard for me to believe that for them. "Okay, you believe," I would say, "but it won't work!"

As time went by, her believing in God began to change me. Gradually I began to confess His promises for our children also. God protected Daniel and his friends when they were teenagers alone in Babylon. Samuel grew up in the religious deadness of Eli's house, and God preserved him. It doesn't matter where our children are or what they are doing. God is bigger than culture, confusion and tragedies. He is still able to preserve our children and protect them. Yes, we have a responsibility to live a righteous life before them and be an example. But that alone is not going to be the answer. Ultimately, we have to live by faith, not by sight. The best thing in the world we can do for our children is to confess God's promises for their lives and believe the Lord for them. And according to our faith it shall be.

I want to encourage you to understand this. It is so important and so crucial that day by day, in every situation, in every way, we choose to walk by faith. I can say from years and years of experience in this journey, those who are willing to take God's Word at face value and act in belief are the ones who experience His promises. But for those who try to explain it, figure it out or work out the promises on their own, there is only defeat.

Conclusion

God wants faith to permeate all of our lives, every moment of every day. He doesn't want us to just fall back on faith when someone is sick and the doctors are unable to help or when the finances are low. Please let us not just use faith when trials or difficulties come our way. Every moment of every day is a time for faith.

Put your life into gear. Believe the promises of God. Step out on faith. Real faith isn't afraid to take a risk. It puts us in places where we can see God in action. Let your faith be alive and active, not dead. Scripture says, "My God shall supply all your need according to His riches in glory by Christ Jesus"

(Philippians 4:19). Don't just say, "I am going to write a better prayer letter and get my support raised." Instead, look at the Scripture and say, "God, You said it!" God honors our faith, whether we have a lot or a little. He gave us the faith in the first place, and He cannot deny Himself. Your willingness to grasp the promises and stake your life on what God said will bring miracles. He is a wonderful God. Take hold of His promises today!

If you see a promise God has made, grasp it in faith. "All things work together for good to those who love God" (Romans 8:28). Take that promise and see beyond the natural circumstances to the substance of things not seen. Grasp the promise in 2 Corinthians about the "light affliction, which is but for a moment . . . working for us a far more exceeding and eternal weight of glory" (2 Corinthians 4:17). Grasp promises for healing. Exodus 15:26 says, "For I am the LORD who heals you." Claim His direction and guidance. "He leads me in the paths of righteousness for His name's sake" (Psalm 23:3).

And when there is no strength in you to lay hold of the promises—when your faith is so low that it seems you cannot go on—praise Him because He is your strength. The best part about living by faith and not by sight is that through it all He supplies everything that we need. He is "the author and finisher of our faith" (Hebrews 12:2). He works with us, never giving up on us. Even when we are so weak that we cannot lift our heads to gaze on that which is invisible, He lifts our heads. Psalm 3:3 says, "But You, O Lord, are a shield for me, my glory and the One who lifts up my head." Faith doesn't come from us—it comes from God.

I pray that somehow you would take God's Word and put your life in a whole different frame of reference. I want you to walk by faith and fix your eyes on the Eternal, Invisible, Almighty God. I want you to be able to say, "You know what? I am going to continue on by faith. Things will work out because my God is an awesome God, and I'm going to trust Him with everything."

If this booklet has been a blessing to you, I would really like to hear from you. You may write to Gospel for Asia, 1800 Golden Trail Court, Carrollton, TX 75010. Or send an email to *kp@gfa.org*.

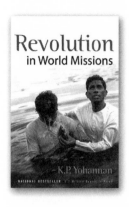

Instill
. . . a passion for the lost.

Impart
. . . fresh zeal for New Testament living.

Stamp
. . . eternity on your eyes.

If you've been blessed by the insight K.P. Yohannan has shared through this booklet, you will want to read *Revolution in World Missions*, his first and most popular book.

When We Have Failed—What Next?

The best *is* yet to come. Do you find that hard to believe? If failure has clouded your vision to see God's redemptive power, this booklet is for you. God's ability to work out His best plan for your life remains. Believe it. (88 pages)

Order online at www.gfa.org

or call 1-800-WIN-ASIA

in Canada 1-888-WIN-ASIA

Booklets by K.P. Yohannan

A Life of Balance
Remember learning how to ride a bike? It was all a matter of
balance. The same is true for our lives. Learn how to develop
that balance, which will keep your life and ministry healthy and
honoring God. (80 pages)

Dependence upon the Lord
Don't build in vain. Learn how to daily depend upon the
Lord—whether in the impossible or the possible—and see your
life bear lasting fruit. (48 pages)

Journey with Jesus
Take this invitation to walk the roads of life intimately with
the Lord Jesus. Stand with the disciples and learn from Jesus'
example of love, humility, power and surrender. (56 pages)

Learning to Pray
Whether you realize it or not, your prayers change things. Be
hindered no longer as K.P. Yohannan shares how you can grow
in your daily prayer life. See for yourself how God still does the
impossible through prayer. (64 pages)

Living by Faith, Not by Sight
The promises of God are still true today: *"Anything is possible to
him who believes!"* This balanced teaching will remind you of
the power of God and encourage you to step out in childlike
faith. (56 pages)

Principles in Maintaining a Godly Organization
Remember the "good old days" in your ministry? This booklet provides a biblical basis for maintaining that vibrancy and
commitment that accompany any new move of God.
(48 pages)

Seeing Him
Do you often live just day-to-day, going through the routine
of life? We so easily lose sight of Him who is our everything.
Through this booklet, let the Lord Jesus restore your heart and
eyes to see Him again. (48 pages)

Stay Encouraged
How are you doing? Discouragement can sneak in quickly and subtly, through even the smallest things. Learn how to stay encouraged in every season of life, no matter what the circumstances may be. (56 pages)

That They All May Be One
In this booklet, K.P. Yohannan opens up his heart and shares from past struggles and real-life examples on how to maintain unity with those in our lives. A must read! (56 pages)

The Beauty of Christ through Brokenness
We were made in the image of Christ that we may reflect all that He is to the hurting world around us. Rise above the things that hinder you from doing this, and see how your life can display His beauty, power and love. (72 pages)

The Lord's Work Done in the Lord's Way
Tired? Burned out? Weary? The Lord's work done in His way will never destroy you. Learn what it means to minister unto Him and keep the holy love for Him burning strong even in the midst of intense ministry. A must-read for every believer! (72 pages)

The Way of True Blessing
What does God value most? Find out in this booklet as K.P. Yohannan reveals truths from the life of Abraham, an ordinary man who became the friend of God. (56 pages)

When We Have Failed—What Next?
The best *is* yet to come. Do you find that hard to believe? If failure has clouded your vision to see God's redemptive power, this booklet is for you. God's ability to work out His best plan for your life remains. Believe it. (88 pages)

Order booklets through:
Gospel for Asia, 1800 Golden Trail Court, Carrollton, TX 75010
Toll free: 1-800-WIN-ASIA
Online: www.gfa.org